Bibliographic information published by the German National Library:

The German National Library lists this publication in the National Bibliography; detailed bibliographic data are available on the Internet at http://dnb.dnb.de .

Imprint:

Copyright © 2003 GRIN Verlag, Open Publishing GmbH
Print and binding: Books on Demand GmbH, Norderstedt Germany
ISBN: 9783640184231

This book at GRIN:

http://www.grin.com/en/e-book/42775/groups-of-charging-for-packaging-waste-are-product-linked-waste-fees-a

Michael A. Braun

Groups of charging for packaging waste. Are product-linked waste fees a more efficient way to reduce waste?

GRIN Publishing

GRIN - Your knowledge has value

Since its foundation in 1998, GRIN has specialized in publishing academic texts by students, college teachers and other academics as e-book and printed book. The website www.grin.com is an ideal platform for presenting term papers, final papers, scientific essays, dissertations and specialist books.

Visit us on the internet:

http://www.grin.com/

http://www.facebook.com/grincom

http://www.twitter.com/grin_com

THREE GROUPS OF CHARGING FOR PACKAGING WASTE IN OVERVIEW – ARE PRODUCT-LINKED WASTE FEES A MORE EFFICIENT WAY TO REDUCE WASTE? – ESSAY BASED ON EXPERIENCES OF THE GERMAN DUALES SYSTEM (GREEN DOT).

Student: Mr. Michael A. Braun

Course: EEM/3 (ERASMUS)

<u>EC 368 A – ENVIRONMENTAL ECONOMICS</u>

THREE GROUPS OF CHARGING FOR PACKAGING WASTE IN OVERVIEW – ARE PRODUCT-LINKED WASTE FEES A MORE EFFICIENT WAY TO REDUCE WASTE? – ESSAY BASED ON EXPERIENCES OF THE GERMAN DUALES SYSTEM (GREEN DOT).

By Michael A. Braun – EEM/3 (ERASMUS)

When consumers buy vegetables on a street market things are normally wrapped in some newspapers. But if they are bought instead from a supermarket next door they are at least covered by some plastic packaging. No wonder people think things are over packaged. (Lascelles, 1996) This essay is going to outline these issues. After a general introduction it focuses on three groups (pre-paid, traditional and innovative)[1] of charging for (mainly packaging) waste that include collection and processing. There will be an evaluation of implications that come up with each method as well. But the emphasis of the essay is on product-linked charging where, as an example, the German Duales System with its Green Dot, is presented more in depth. This method is widely seen as helpful for the environment because it caused both significant reductions of the quantities but also innovations within the manufacturing and packaging sector as well. Therefore product-linked charging might be seen as an efficient way to less waste. For further reading and a clear structure of the essay a short view on references and appendixes in the end is recommended.

Talking about packaging waste (plastics, glass, papers, metals, …) society is facing a tricky problem. (Tietenberg, 1998) Because it is not clear whether this kind of waste is useless or useful in the end of the day. In other words whether it is an economic good or bad. Of course packaging waste can be seen as positive. It keeps diverse goods clean and safe, so they are ready for transport and sale. After having done its task packaging can be a huge generator of new raw materials within the recycling process. Therefore it is necessary to collect, sort and process it. And this task needs a lot of employees and opens up new markets with all supporting industries. In this line of argument, waste coming from packaging can try to solve its own market failure. (Bastian, 2001) On the other hand waste always has something negative on it. Pollution costs that are not included in its price are hard to manage and expensive for society. Also the use and finiteness of resources has to be taken into account as well as problems coming up with scare disposal capacities. For these reasons politics try

---

[1] There is a range of different points of view. This grouping is not widely agreed. Moreover, it is a very individual idea of an solution.

to come to a reduction of packaging quantity. By giving incentives both customers and producers are forced to change their behaviour significantly. One should act in a more innovative way that saves money in the long-run. And the other one should have a stronger look for products that are more environmental friendly.

Because it is not clear which side weights more, politics do have a massive problem to deal with. Of course sustainability and environmental factors have to be taken into account[2] but on the other side this market failure generates problems to consumers and manufacturers or generally spoken the society. Question is how to act with a good in the end that does neither have a real use nor a scarceness as well. And, if there is none who wants to benefit from it, who is responsible for it? Who takes care about all consequences coming up – consumers, enterprises or society? This essay is not going to solve such questions but tries to give a general idea about different ways of charging for packaging waste. Therefore it seems to be necessary to have a better understanding about the topic first.

According to Bates & Phillips (1998; B&P) or Tietenberg (1998; the three 'R') waste management could be divided into a clear hierarchy. The priority (1) always should lay on reduction of the quantity of waste at source. Then (2) follows the reuse of materials and objects. This means putting them back so they do not enter the waste stream at all. Later (3) recovery of value or energy from waste materials is recommended. Only as a last option (4) disposal (landfill or incineration) can be seen as an option. But nowadays incineration is not very unpopular; the method is linked to health problems and does hardly improve society's environmental responsibility. And traditionally, a lot of the waste quantities have been land filled. However, this procedure is getting more and more expensive for several reasons. On one hand, landfill capacities are closed for environmental reasons and on the other hand, the left capacities are becoming seriously scarce. Further on current legislation all over Europe forces the waste management process outlined above in terms of the given hierarchy. Legal obligations such as landfill taxes are introduced and will become probably much more relevant in future as well. One of their aims is always to reduce the final quantity of waste for disposal and to increase recycling and reuse rates significantly. Because it is mostly believed that waste reduction and recycling are the only sustainable solutions, they also should encourage a waste minimisation in general. (McGurty, 1994) Therefore enterprises, households and public institutions should try to reduce their quantities on the long-run. For enterprises it can be assumed that a clear environmental management strategy can cause high financial savings as well as it gives a environmental friendly image in customers view.

Moreover, costs (not only monetary) caused by waste are much higher than usually assumed. They are not only the price that has to be paid to get rid of it. Again, B&P (1998; according to MCG, 1997) say costs can generally be split into two main parts: the visible and the hidden costs. In the first section solid, liquid and special waste, gaseous emissions and by-products to tackle with can be found. These are the most obvious costs. But hidden costs are high and relevant as well. They cover energy and processing inefficiencies, unrealised production capacities and re-work, lost revenue and reduced profits as well as purchase costs of materials. When all these factors are taken into consideration it becomes clear that disposal costs are only one part of the bill. On the other hand costs for waste management itself should be separated into two parts as well. They do not only cover the process of collection but also further tasks. These could be the preparation for reuse or recycling (cleaning, sorting, transportation, …) as well as disposal affairs.

But how could the government handle these problems? How can innovative ideas for waste management, that are not always easy to accept, be introduced successfully? It is widely agreed (different references) that only strong political support as well as education and information campaigns can do this. And the system has to have a high degree of reliability and cost-effectiveness. To gain stable acceptance political forces should provide benefits for both consumers and manufacturers to reduce the quantity of waste. Directly and clear linked fees can help to get into the right direction. As outlined earlier the strategy according to B&P and Tietenberg should be a clear hierarchy. Therefore most of the charging systems that are discussed following (N.N., 2000) do force consumers and producers to reduce the quantity of waste as well as they try to solve the problem of disposal. Nevertheless there can be found a wide range of charging schemes[3]. Most surprising in this context might be the fact that they are running successfully in a lot of different countries within different cultures and under different local conditions. Sometimes they are designed to cover costs and sometimes only for partial cost recovery.

When it comes to the introduction of any new waste management system Jenkins (1993) recommends to be tolerant with several challenges coming up in this period of time. There might be a adverse reaction of the target group (consumers of the waste management service) because of a lack of understanding. Sometimes some behavioural changes can be seen as well and, mostly only for a short period of time, an increase of illegal waste tipping is

---

[2] Often they are not that relevant within the process of decision-making. Also a lack of information and time lags in adoption of new technologies do cause serious problems of waste. Or in other words there might be too much packaging. (Lascelles, 1996)

[3] A general differentiation might be the way of payment. Some (flat annual fees, volume-based, frequency-based, waste bag, tag or sticker, product-linked) have to be paid up-front. But others (weight-based, volume-based, frequency-based) do charge afterwards.

reported. In general it is necessary to have a high degree of participation within the relevant group but this often can lead to a significant reduction of the quantity of waste.

The first group (N.N., 2000; appendix 2) of charging for waste to mention is the 'pre-paid section' that contains two different schemes, waste bags and tags or stickers. In the waste bag scheme the waste collector picks up only special bags that were purchased earlier from the council or dedicated retailers. A problem within this scheme might be the matter of the bags that become part of the waste stream, and bags normally might be not strong enough to prevent serious damages (kids, animals, accidents,…). The tag or sticker scheme works nearly the same way. However, here customers have got their own bins. To be emptied a special purchased tag or sticker has to be bought and pressed on the bin. The problem is that this sign could be lost or stolen. Charging within the pre-paid group is easy to introduce and therefore the scheme is mostly used in the U.S. where it is often combined with a frequency-based collection. The advantage for councils might be the purchase up-front which creates a significant time gap, this means money comes in today but is paid for future services. Therefore customers are really aware of waste (volume) reduction for which they have got a clear incentive - to save their own money. Within this scheme it is very easy to be flexible. For a higher amount of waste customers only have to buy more pre-paid colleting signs.

The second group (N.N., 2000; appendix 2) generates much more work for everyone. The 'traditional section' has got two, very similar, ways of charging for waste. One is the volume-based, the other one the frequency-based way of charging. This scheme is the most popular in the western world, apart from not paying anything of course. It often is a combination of both and says 'less is cheaper' as a general guideline to its users. This becomes clearer by having a look at the schemes in detail. In both ways the user has to make decisions. These will be valid for a specific period of time and allow a specific amount of waste into the waste management process. The volume-based variant offers a variety of different bins, mostly two to four sizes between 50 and 240 litres. It is difficult to forecast what size might be to right one. Once a size is in customers use over the chosen period of time there is no clear incentive to have less waste than the bin could contain. Additionally the bins have to have a special size so they can be collected with a automated collection system. This makes it easy to collect but council has to verify whether a bin is allowed to be emptied or not. Therefore often specific tags have to be pressed on the bins. The frequency-based scheme basically works the same. Only not the size of the bins but time of empty has to be chosen. Payments have to be made up-front as well. Because of this there is no real incentive to reduce waste. However, to save money users might tend to have a low frequency, but this later could cause health problems so it might be not the best. Within the frequency-based way there are two sub-schemes, the fixed-period and the fully flexible. The first one is basically discussed above. The second one (so called 'as-needs'-basis) always allows the users individually to decide whether a bin should be emptied or not. Therefore the price that has to be paid is variable. Users get a greater incentive to reduce their amount of waste but council might face problems with planning and organising.

Within the third group (N.N., 2000; appendix 2), the 'innovative section', there are also two schemes: the weight-based and the product-linked. The first one usually involves the use of special collection vehicles that have got some automated weight-recording equipment on board. This records the relevant data for each single bin. Therefore the system is expensive (high up-front costs for council), difficult to introduce and time-consuming. Also the measurement of weight is not accurate under all circumstances and there are huge concerns about security of personal related data as well, but each waste reduction will be measured and reported soon a strong incentive to reduce the amount of waste is given. This method might be seen as one of the most fairest ways to charge for waste at all; although this it is introduced only in few regions. The other one's product-linked charging schemes. This idea was first introduced in Germany.[4] A main characteristic is that this system is paid indirectly. This means customers do not have to pay for collection and processing itself. Fees are included in the price of the original product covered by its particular packaging. Therefore this scheme does not need any bins because it works with own bags, similar to the waste bags in the pre-paid section.

But what were the reasons for introduction of such innovative system? For Germany since 1991 the German Packaging Ordinance makes private industries responsible for collecting, sorting, and recycling of packaging waste that they have generated. When it became clear that the government had decided to regulate packaging waste, industry lobbied for the start of a private run collection and recovery system. (Bernhardt, 1992) Result was the Duales System Deutschland GmbH (DSD), a nation-wide system for collection of used sales packages. The company was established as a non-profit organization in the beginning by about 600 businesses. By the end of 2000 there were over 19.000 members in the system engaged and, according to the annual report of this year, it processed 5,48m tons (approx. 78kg/capita) of packaging and generated a turnover of over DEM 4bn. (N.N., 2001)

Since this law, German retailers are required to take back all materials for goods they sold, but if they belong to the system they are exempt from this. In the DSD waste-handling

---

[4] Later can be a more detailed overview of the scheme find.

scheme, retailers are charged for belonging to it. Similarly, producers of packaging have to pay a fee that is based on the volume and weight of potential waste they produce. For this reasons enterprises do have strong incentives for reducing packaging. This behaviour cause surprising results: today companies do often have less costs for packaging than before DSD - although they do pay fees! (Micklitz, 1992) Only implementation of new innovations for less waste lead to this. But most of all the objective of the law was to avoid waste – and all waste which cannot be avoided has to be recycled. This target was reached as well because of significant reduction of double-wrappings and not necessary packaging at all. To divide between packaging that belongs to the scheme or not a small Green Dot marks everything that uses DSD-registered material to encourage consumers to purchase recyclable materials. This label indicates also that this particular packaging may not be returned to the retailer but should be put into specially dedicated collection containers (yellow bags/bins; appendix), and it also says that all costs are included in product-price.

According to the DSD annual report 2000 Germany is worldwide one of the leading countries in managing solid waste, especially in recycling of packaging waste. However, the German legislation and the scheme itself as well are criticized for being ecologically and economically inefficient. (Schroll, 1999) Germany's high recycling quotas have led to very high costs in an ineffective waste management system (only few recycling capacities). But the results of the system are mixed. Huge packaging reductions, figures do vary between 20% and 70% (several references), and innovations have been achieved but citizen participation, which is voluntary in the scheme, has been so enthusiastic that volumes collected are 3-4 times more of what was expected. Now the DSD has become overburdened with collected waste, for which there is not enough capacities in Germany. In addition, the scheme faced financial problems as many enterprises (free riders) had put Green Dots on their products but have not paid the required fees. (Kulik, 1993)

Overall because of the systems great success nowadays twelve European countries are using the Green Dot trademark actively. And since 2000/2001 four non-EU states, Norway, Latvia, Hungary and the Czech Republic, joined the scheme as well. If this way of managing waste can play the leading role in EU's future is not clear yet, but might be a serious option. For sure: this process needs a lot of time to match all the different national systems. But the Green Dot is the most widely used trademark all over the world yet; meanwhile it can be found on over 460bn pieces of packaging. Problems that came up in the beginning of DSD are now on the way to being solved, showing the system has matured. (Prudent, 2002)

But which implications might the problem of packaging waste has for politics? What are the key issues that come up by linking all theoretical ideas from the beginning of this essay with the different ways of charging for waste? And how can these fit with the experiences made in Germany? It can be realised that there is a strong desire to force the reduction of waste in general, not only for ethical but also for clear business reasons. And especially in Germany DSD has shown the high acceptance of the population. On the other hand, strictly following this hierarchy, would mean to start with reduction first, moving on to reuse and than to recycling. Of course B&P's and Tietenbergs hierarchy is well introduced in Germany. But as a critique it can be argued the reuse-part is nearly left out within the Green Dot scheme. Although there is a huge deposit area, DSD does not support it for own reasons. Moreover, this scheme really does gain of having one-time packaging that goes into yellow bags and bins. And there might be another critique: high costs coming with this way of managing waste do generate huge welfare losses for society. Because of this state-introduced collection and recycling scheme a inefficient resource allocation can be indicated. DSD is the only provider of such service in Germany, therefore they are a monopoly. And most of the authors (several references) argue that not gains but losses because of size do come up. This is not a problem for society in general but one for the consumers of products that are packed – to be honest: nevertheless the whole society. And as a last critique it can be said such monopoly generates a massive barrier of entry. Not for competitors in the waste market but for manufacturers of consumer goods for the German market. If they do not know how to manage waste they are not allowed to enter the market.

To conclude the essay it might be good to compress some important points shortly. Whether waste is an economic good or bad is already not clear decided – and probably can not as well. Unfortunately this depends on a lot of different assumptions that have to be made always new and also the way how a system is installed. But as a main thesis can be seen the 'hierarchy theory' that focuses on R's – reduction, reuse, recycling and recovery. The priority of reduction is in most of the western countries accepted, and only the transformation into practical guidelines and legislation needs to be improved sometimes. For a successful introduction of such organized waste management system according to several mentioned authors it is necessary to have strong political support as well a support of all touched groups of society. To gain this, especially of consumers, information and education helps. Moreover, clear benefits for businesses have to be provided so that they are encouraged to invest in new technologies and innovation. Therefore indeed related to the experiences made with DSD and Green Dot in Germany it can be said that product-linked fees for waste do cause a reduction of waste for disposal and do lead to less output of packaging in general as well.

Maybe consumers will come back to the mentioned example in the beginning. Maybe not only vegetables but also a lot of different other things might be purchased in future in the way street markets did and do work. Maybe customers do bring their own packaging to shops – and can save money therefore. Or delivery services do bring goods to households. It is not clear, but only the way waste management has to work: reduction of the quantity of resources and as much reuse, recycling and recovery as possible.

References

BASTIAN. N. 2001. *Im Kampf um den Verpackungsmuell kommt die Regierung unter Zugzwang.* In: dpa (Europadienst), 28.11.2001. Available from: Genios Wirtschaftsdatenbanken [Accessed 22.11.2002]

BATES, M. & PHILLIPS, P. 1998. *Waste minimisation in the food and drink industry.* In: Nutrition & Food Science, Nov./Dec. 1998, Nr. 6, pp.330-334. Available on the UAD CD-ROM collection [Accessed 29.11.2002]

BERNHARDT, K. 1992. *Germany's new packaging laws: The 'Green Dot' arrives.* In: Business America, 24.02.1992, Vol. 113, Iss. 4, pp.36-37. Available from: ABI/Inform Select [Accessed 06.11.2002]

BROWN-HUMES, C. 1994. *Running on rubbish.* In: Financial Times, 04.05.1994. Available on the UAD CD-ROM collection [Accessed 29.11.2002]

CAIRNCROSS, F. 1993. *Waste and the environment: A lasting reminder.* In: The Economist, 29.05.1993, Vol. 327, Iss. 7813, p.3. Available from: ABI/Inform Select [Accessed 06.11.2002]

CAIRNCROSS, F. 1992. *How Europe's companies reposition to recycle.* In: Harvard Business Review, Mar/Apr 1992, Vol. 70, Iss. 2, pp.34-42. Available from: ABI/Inform Select [Accessed 06.11.2002]

CHYNOWETH, E. 1993. *Plastics struggle to meet recycling targets in Europe.* In: Chemical Week, 25.08.1993, Vol. 153, Iss. 7, p.33. Available from: ABI/Inform Select [Accessed 06.11.2002]

CHYNOWETH, E. 1993. *Plastics waste trashes German recycling scheme.* In: Chemical Week, 30.06.1993, Vol. 152, Iss. 25, p.18. Available from: ABI/Inform Select [Accessed 06.11.2002]

CHYNOWETH, E. 1993. *Recycling: German efforts seen as a threat.* In: Chemical Week, 17.02.1993, Vol. 152, Iss. 6, p.20. Available from: ABI/Inform Select [Accessed 06.11.2002]

JENKINS, R. 1993. *The economics of solid waste reduction.* Cheltenham: Edward Elgar.

KENNETT, J. 1993. *Manufacturers should heed German lessons in retail 'take-back' programs.* In: Environment Today, Dec. 1993, Vol. 4, Iss. 12, pp. 35. Available from: ABI/Inform Select [Accessed 06.11.2002]

KULIK, A. 1994. *German recycling system braces for changes in 1994.* In: World Wastes, Jan. 1994, Vol. 37, Iss. 1, pp.8-9. Available from: ABI/Inform Select [Accessed 06.11.2002]

KULIK, A. 1993. *German waste disposal evolves under new laws.* In: World Wastes, Sep. 1993, Vol. 36, Iss. 9, pp.16-17. Available from: ABI/Inform Select [Accessed 06.11.2002]

KULIK, A. 1993. *Differing recycling symbols confuse German consumers.* In: World wastes, Feb. 1993, Vol. 36, Iss. 2, pp.14-16. Available from: ABI/Inform Select [Accessed 06.11.2002]

LASCELLES, D. 1996. *Taking the rap on wrapping.* In: Financial Times, 31.01.1996. Available on the UAD CD-ROM collection [Accessed 29.11.2002]

LASCELLES, D. 1995. *Time to take charge of waste.* In: Financial Times, 17.05.1995. Available on the UAD CD-ROM collection [Accessed 29.11.2002]

MCGURTY, F. 1994. *Less is more – Manufacturers are trying to cut their use of packaging materials.* In: Financial Times, 07.12.1994. Available on the UAD CD-ROM collection [Accessed 29.11.2002]

MICKLITZ, H.-W. 1992. *The German packaging order: A model for state-induced waste.* In: Columbia Journal of World Business, Fall 1992/Winter 1993, Vol. 27, Iss. 3, pp.120-127. Available from: ABI/Inform Select [Accessed 06.11.2002]

PRUDENT, C. 2002. *Kostenfaktor Gruener Punkt.* In: Impulse, 01.08.2002, Nr. 8, p.80. Available from: Genios Wirtschaftsdatenbanken [Accessed 22.11.2002]

ROBERTS, M. 1996. *Germany beats recycling targets.* In: Chemical Week, 05.06.1996, Vol. 158, Iss. 22, p.22. Available from: ABI/Inform Select [Accessed 06.11.2002]

SCHROLL, M. 1999. *Mandatory recycling, but at what cost?* In: Waste Age, Apr. 1999, Vol. 30, Iss. 4, pp.20-21. Available from: ABI/Inform Select [Accessed 06.11.2002]

STERN, M. 1993. *Is this the ultimate in recycling?* In: Across the board, May 1993, Vol. 30, Iss. 4, pp.28-31. Available from: ABI/Inform Select [Accessed 06.11.2002]

TIETENBERG, T. 1998. *Environmental economics and policy.* 2nd edition. Reading, MA: Addison-Wesley

WILSHER, P. 1993. *Rubbish rules the day.* In: Management Today, Sep. 1993, pp.20-21. Available from: ABI/Inform Select [Accessed 06.11.2002]

N.N. 2002. *Position paper on waste disposal charging.* Hong Kong General Chamber of Commerce, May 2002. Available on the World Wide Web: http://www.chamber.org.hk/ memberarea/chamber_view/environment/landfill.asp [Accessed 29.11.2002]

N.N. 2001. *Duales System klagt in Luxemburg wegen Verpackungsgebuehren.* In: dpa (Europadienst), 04.07.2001. Available from: Genios Wirtschaftsdatenbanken [Accessed 22.11.2002]

N.N. 2000. *Local authority waste charging scheme – Best practise evaluation study.* Enviros Aspinwall, Edinburgh on behalf of the Scotland and Northern Ireland Forum for environmental research (SNIFFER), Jul. 2000. Available on the World Wide Web: http://www.sepa.org.uk/nws/pdf/r_and_d/sniffer_waste_charging_study.pdf [Accessed 29.11.2002]

N.N. 1994. *Clean up your own mess.* In: Canadian Business, Jan. 1994, Vol. 67, Iss. 1, pp.24-25. Available from: ABI/Inform Select [Accessed 06.11.2002]

N.N. 1993. *German systems success swaps plastics recycling efforts, threatens change for Europe.* In: Chemical & Engineering News, 04.10.1993, Vol. 71, Iss. 40, pp.12-13. Available from: ABI/Inform Select [Accessed 06.11.2002]

N.N. 1992. *diverse.* In: COKER, A. & RICHARDS, C. (ed.). *Valuing the environment.* London: Belhaven Press

N.N. 1991. *Recycling in Germany: A wall of waste.* In: The Economist, 30.11.1991, Vol. 321, Iss. 7735, p.73. Available from: ABI/Inform Select [Accessed 06.11.2002]

Bag or tag / sticker - strengths

• Easy to implement and operate and provides direct incentive for waste reduction
• Allows residents full flexibility
• Simple billing system
• No special arrangements necessary for multi-occupancy buildings
• Sealed bags/sacks prevent use by other persons
• Tidy streets (bag systems) - no empty bins on streets

Bag or tag / sticker - weaknesses

• Bags/sacks require manual collection; not compatible with automatic collection systems
• Refuse easily scattered from damaged bags
• Possible loss of tags/stickers
• Unstable revenue stream
• May encourage residents to store waste for excessive time
• Plastic sacks included in waste stream - use of bags may be seen as retrograde step

Volume-based - strengths

• Easy to install in areas that already use wheeled bins and automatic uplift systems
• Fairly stable revenue stream and allows flexibility in design of waste collection charges

Volume-based - weaknesses

• Problems with selection of a suitable bin size - resulting in Council having to replace bins
• Limited by range of bins sizes - fixed annual charge removes incentive to reduce waste
• High up-front capital costs
• Multi-occupancy dwellings
• Complex billing process – requires tracking of bins by address / checking during collection
• Waste cramming by residents

Frequency based (fixed period) - strengths

• Direct financial incentive to residents
• Easy to implement and operate - requires simple changes to billing system
• Low capital cost - by using existing bins
• May result in significant reductions in collection time (and costs)
• Fairly stable revenue stream

Frequency based (fixed period) - weaknesses

• Public health and amenity concerns - from waste storing
• Fixed annual charge removes week-to-week incentive to reduce waste
• Staff must ensure that chosen frequency has been paid for
• Waste cramming by residents

Frequency based (fully flexible) - strengths

• Allows residents full flexibility
• Provides direct incentives
• Requires no judgement by collections staff
• Automated billing system
• Low cost - by using existing bins

Frequency based (fully flexible) - weaknesses

• Public health and amenity concerns - may be higher
• Costs of transponders and associated equipment - to record uplifts
• Difficulties associated with installing transponders (existing bins) and matching addresses
• Relatively unstable revenue stream
• Waste cramming - by householders

Weight-based - strengths

• Allows residents full flexibility
• Provides direct incentives
• Requires no judgement by collections staff
• Flexible, automated billing approach
• Generates good data for decision making in waste management

Weight-based - weaknesses

• Expensive to set up – requires installation of sophisticated weighing equipment
• Possible inaccuracies in data logging process
• May be significant increase in collection times (care required in weighing process)
• May encounter higher levels of community opposition
• More susceptible to problems associated with waste illegally placed in other peoples bins

Written on the basis of N.N. 2000. *Local authority waste charging scheme – Best practise evaluation study.* Enviros Aspinwall, Edinburgh on behalf of the Scotland and Northern Ireland Forum for environmental research (SNIFFER), Jul. 2000. Available on the World Wide Web: http://www.sepa.org.uk/nws/pdf/r_and_d/sniffer_waste_charging_study.pdf   [Accessed 29.11.2002]